Praise for *Sell Without*

The thought of mingling with strangers at a networking event makes my stomach turn... In Stephanie's new book, I learned how to better prepare myself for talking about my business without sounding salesy... I'm ready for my next networking opportunity—bring it on!

Brandy Whalen, Founder of Whalen Media

Sell Without Being Salesy is a must-have book for anyone in the professional services industry who wants to attract clients in an authentic way. There are many books that teach sales tactics, but few teach us how to build powerful relationships that result in sales without feeling pushy or salesy in the process. Stephanie shows you how to do just that!

Jessica Nazarali, CEO of Jessica Nazarali Consulting

Sell Without Being Salesy is a great read with direct, specific advice. The talking point suggestions are immediately applicable. Reading this book makes attending business gatherings much more enjoyable and purposeful. I appreciate Stephanie's understanding of the value of authenticity.

Laura Alms, Founder Attorney, Alms Law Offices, Denver, Colorado

The knowledge and perspective that Stephanie has compiled in this book is a must have for any professional service provider looking to create more long-lasting strategic business relationships.

Rob Grabil, President, Chief Executive Network

Stephanie is spot-on with her advice for professional service providers. We are not door-to-door salesmen. We need to foster the long-lasting trust and confidence of our clients. This book gave me clarity on how to do that in a natural, authentic way. I especially enjoyed the tips on adjusting my mindset going into conferences and networking events.

Rose Standifer, Attorney

Stephanie Wachman demystifies the conundrum of sales talk and technique with practical steps that move the reader away from the complicated and into the simplicity of what the sale is really about.

Jon Khoury, Executive Director of Cottonwood Center for the Arts

Sell Without Being Salesy

Sell Without Being Salesy

Stephanie Wachman

Symetree Strategies
Denver, Colorado
www.stephaniewachman.com

First Edition: August 2019

The publisher is not responsible for websites (or their content) that are not owned by the publisher.

ISBN Print Version: 978-0-578-52583-9
ISBN Ebook: 978-0-578052584-6

Cover Design: James Clarke

1. Business 2. Sales 3. Networking

Printed in the United States of America

Contents

Acknowledgements

I dedicate this book to my father, who has since left this world. He taught me everything I know about building relationships. My father was an incredible businessman and salesman who owned a packaging company in Montreal, Canada. He traveled across Canada regularly and befriended his customers. Nobody ever had anything but positive and kind words to say about my dad. By watching him, I learned the value of relationships.

I also dedicate this book to my mother, Arlene, who worked alongside my father. In addition to supporting my dad in his relationships, she built a large network of her own.

To my husband, David Maginsky, for all his help, guidance, support, and direction.

To my kids, Joshua and Benjamin, for always being my cheering committee. To my brother and sister, Jeff and Lynn, for ongoing support and guidance throughout my life.

And to my clients who have affirmed the value of relationships by openly sharing their struggles and challenges. I wrote this book for you because I sincerely want to provide you the wins you need to keep building.

Introduction

Most professional service providers—lawyers, accountants, architects, and consultants—learn the fundamentals of sales by reading books and taking courses. But they rarely learn about the steps they should take *before* they are in a position to make a sale.

That is a problem, because what happens before a sale—if done correctly—can greatly increase the effectiveness of the actual selling.

This book is designed to help you think clearly about how to develop a pre-sales plan that opens the doors to new sales opportunities *in a natural way*.

Here's my premise. People like to make business referrals when they know and trust the person they are dealing with. Business grows because of high-quality, long-lasting relationships. But, as I've observed during my extensive career as a former sales professional and business development trainer, most professionals never learn how to build and sustain these relationships. As a result, they often miss out on large and fruitful opportunities.

In my experience and observation, most professionals buy books about sales techniques and sign up for sales courses to help them, well . . . sell.

However, they primarily learn about "consultative sales." This old selling model requires the salesperson to spend a lot of energy trying to understand the prospective customer's problems and needs, and then figure out how to solve those problems.

I have found this to be a tired model, one that frequently puts salespeople in the awkward position of not coming across as natural or authentic. Many of my clients say they have a hard time with this approach because it makes them feel like a pushy salesperson who follows a formula. I don't blame them. It's even harder for my clients who must sell their own services rather than a company's products. Let's face it, self-promotion is uncomfortable.

Many popular sales training methods are formulaic and not designed to help people sell in an authentic way that protects the *quality* of prospective business relationships. Rather, these methods force us to use gimmicky techniques designed to convince and cajole people into buying a service or product.

My least favorite method teaches salespeople how to handle objections to a sales pitch. It sounds something like this: "If money weren't a problem, would you use my services?" Or, "Should we schedule a meeting with your boss now to cover any of the objections he or she might have?" These outdated methods force us to be "salesy" to get the business. They require us to use an approach that is contrived instead of natural.

My clients want to know how to grow their businesses without feeling like they are selling used cars. They want to feel confident and authentic without being pushy or salesy. In short, they want to be themselves.

Moreover, every consumer today can see what your firm or company has to offer just by going to a website. They don't need much more information directly from you about your services. Thus, the key to business development isn't information; it's relational authenticity. Therefore, if you don't know how to be yourself while building and sustaining real relationships, then whatever sales approach you adopt will be awkward.

This book will show you how to work with your natural strengths and how to use those as your foundation for improving your business development skills.

If those of us who work in professional services could get comfortable with business development and see it as an opportunity to build authentic relationships, then the word *sales* could be dropped completely. We could approach each contact as an opportunity to *serve* our clients and prospective clients, rather than a high-pressure requirement to *impose* our services on them in pushy or salesy ways. By sincerely helping them, we can generate business within a strong relational network. Growth will naturally flow toward us. We won't need to chase after it.

During my professional sales career, which continues to this day, I have attended more training sessions then I can count. I've had people record my practice sales calls on video and then use those videos (VHS recordings, in those days) to critique my work. If you want a discomforting experience, try watching yourself on a mock sales call. I watched myself turn red and fumble through pitches as my role-playing prospects challenged me with questions and objections. I've had bosses tag along with me on sales calls to give me critical feedback, and I've had supervisors observe my telephone sales calls.

Through all this, I've learned that there is a clear difference between selling a product and selling a service. When selling a product, you are merely conveying information about its features and benefits. You are just the messenger. However, as a service provider, you are selling your services, which are based on your personal and professional experiences, knowledge, education, and reputation.

That distinction makes a big difference. I've learned that pounding the pavement the traditional way is not an ideal approach for professional service providers. Instead, they need to think about the value they bring to every conversation and every interaction. Selling your services shouldn't be about hustling; it should be about showcasing your knowledge and expertise in a manner that authentically aligns who you are all the time with your clients and prospects.

The work of business development might feel uncomfortable at first, but if you keep it real and build one relationship at a time, then you will see ongoing opportunities for new business.

Start fresh with this book. There is a way to build your business by learning how to develop high-quality, high-trust relationships that will benefit you, your firm, and your prospective clients. This book is designed to help you build and maintain business relationships in a natural way that fits with your strengths and personality, and, if you work for an organization or firm, your colleagues' strengths too.

As I describe in this book, developing future business opportunities depends on the first moments of interaction between people at networking events and other business interactions. I'll teach you how to handle those initial meetings.

You also need to *sustain* long-term relationships. Doing that requires patience and consistency. Sometimes it can take years for business opportunities to present themselves. But if you always nurture and grow those relationships, many will lead to new work with people you like and who become your ideal clients. So, I'll show you how to follow up with new contacts, and how to take care of long-term clients.

If you are tired of "selling yourself," if you don't know how to begin to grow your business, if you are frustrated because your practice isn't growing, if you're not sure how to contribute to the success of your firm and increase revenue, then this book will be your guide to doing all of that—in your own, natural way.

Sell Without Being Salesy

Chapter One

Developing a Habit of Business Development

HubSpot shows that nine out of ten buying decisions are based on personal recommendations. To be specific, 92 percent of buyers trust referrals from people they know. So, it's important to think about who you know and who you need to know in order to start building strong relationships.

These numbers also demonstrate why people who provide professional services—lawyers and accountants, to name a few—need to grow business through trusting, high-quality relationships.

As professional service providers, we don't sell products; we sell our abilities and our services. Therefore, prospective clients find it harder to compare us online to other providers. They can't evaluate us as they would when buying a computer. Rather, they base their decisions on how we communicate. They evaluate our knowledge, experience, reputation, interactions, and ability to relate. This means that our relational abilities will set us apart from our competition. The key is knowing how to build relationships, consistently.

Be Committed

The first step in building your relationship network is to understand that business development takes long-term, constant commitment. It's not a spigot that you turn off and on. If you aren't regularly and consistently working at developing high-quality relationships, then you won't get the results you hope for.

Your commitment to business development should become a habit, like brushing your teeth every morning. Both are great habits that lead to positive results. With consistent practice, you'll just do it without even thinking about it. So, I encourage you to make your business relationships a priority. Don't allow other work pressures to suppress the time you spend to develop new contacts and to maintain strong connections with your existing clients.

Start by creating a weekly habit of business

development. Take little steps. I have a friend and colleague who used to say, "If you commit to floss just one tooth a day, chances are you will floss them all." Small steps can lead to lasting behavior change. Pick a day or two every week and block out that time in your calendar. If you have an assistant, have that person help you stay on task every week, or set up a reminder in your calendar. Gradually, you'll develop a behavior and habit around marketing and business development. Consistently making time for this is a "rainmaking" secret.

When I worked in sales for a uniform service provider, I had to make two hundred phone calls, knock on thirty doors, and make at least fifteen face-to-face calls every week. This was a traditional, "salesy" selling model. (If you feel yourself getting uneasy, you can breathe a sigh of relief because that is not what I recommend.) I learned from that experience that (a) I hated making phone calls to people I didn't know; and (b) I didn't feel quite as awful and awkward making calls on Fridays as I did on Mondays because the weekend was near. I think everyone, me included, seemed more relaxed on Fridays. So, I settled into the routine of Friday phone calls, which proved to be a successful model that fit me, my personality, and my sales quota.

I encourage you to build your schedule in a way that allows you to consistently work on business development in a comfortable way—a way that helps you not burn out and give up. By developing a natural cadence for this important work, you will get results that you can track. Then you can adjust as needed.

The second aspect of developing this habit is to know how to make the best use of that time. If you sit down at your desk on a Wednesday morning and only *think* about who you are going to call or meet, then nothing much will happen. When you work on business development, you should be ready to take *action*, to execute your plan. You should not be using that time to wonder about who you'd like to speak to. Therefore, be deliberate about planning to connect with people ahead of time. If you don't, your results will be mediocre. Even an hour each week is better than nothing. But remember that business development is a numbers game. Your opportunities grow with the amount of networking you do. So, spend at least two hours per week and see what the results look like. Your ability to bring in new clients is directly linked to how many relationships you nurture.

Get Off the Roller Coaster

If you're like most busy professionals, the intense demands of your business will delude you into thinking you don't have time to develop future business relationships. However, you can't provide your services if you don't have any clients. And without a substantial and strong business network—relationships that you nourish and care for in personal ways—you will soon find yourself struggling to develop your business.

In fact, you could find yourself riding a financial roller coaster. Consider what happens to people who ride the The Gravity Max, one of the scariest roller coaster rides in the world. Located in Lihpao Land Discovery World in Taiwan, this roller coaster is *terrifying*. Riders are locked in a car that is pulled by a chain 115 feet to the top, where it balances on a horizontal platform. The entire structure then tilts downward until the coaster is completely vertical. Once released, the cars connect with another track that drops thirty-four stories. The coaster reaches nearly sixty miles per hour, blasts through a tunnel, and completes a 360-degree inside loop before winding its way to the finish. Just thinking about it makes my heart beat out of my chest.

It's the same feeling I get when there is a full bank account one day and an empty one the next day—with no sign of where new business is coming from.

Some people love roller coasters like The Gravity Max, but the financial roller coaster just causes a lot of fear and screaming without any of the fun. It happens like this: You start out with great clients. You bring in $20 thousand to $30 thousand per month. It's all good. You're riding high. That thrill leads you to falsely believe that your clients are keeping you too busy to do regular business development.

However, at the top of the roller coaster, you finish all your work for a client who had given you a retainer worth $15 thousand a month. You realize that you need to find a new client to fill that gap. Then you say to yourself, *Uh oh! Where am I going to find a client who can pay me that much on retainer? I better start going to networking meetings again.* That's when you feel like you're in freefall.

Let's say that you sign a contract with a new client. *Everything's good. I've got a great client again.* This time the retainer is $7 thousand a month. You're down about 50 percent compared to what you had, and business isn't growing, but at least you're paying the bills again.

The new client starts taking a lot of your time, of course. And, again, you conclude that you don't have enough time for networking. You're too busy to meet people for coffee or to attend networking events and conferences.

Suddenly you remember that you have to pay a staggering sum in quarterly taxes. You set out to find another client to make up the difference. *Time to start networking again . . .*

This happened to one of my clients, an attorney who is a litigator. She was very busy doing depositions, working on a huge case, and travelling. I remember her saying, "I really don't have time to do any networking or business development right now." A few months later, I received a panicked call from her. She said, "I just settled the big case I was working on only to realize that I don't have any other opportunities in my pipeline."

As you can see, it's very easy to push business development to the side when your practice gets busy. I know from experience. The problem is, you can't be 100 percent sure that you will be busy all the time. That's why it is so important to stay committed to business development consistently—as a habit—*especially* when you get busy. Otherwise you'll soon have that terrifying experience of plunging from the top of the roller coaster to the bottom. You'll realize that you have nothing going on.

The best way to ensure a successful long-term pipeline of business is to network all the time, especially when work is on an upward trajectory. Keep in mind that it typically takes six months to a year to solidify a business relationship, build trust, and get a referral. So, the foundation of a successful business depends on your commitment to develop solid relationships.

In the next chapter, I address a barrier that often prevents people from connecting with others: *fear*.

Chapter Two

Overcoming the Fear of Networking

We've established that being committed to regular business development is crucial, a foundation to your success. Building high quality relationships is the key.

A primary way we can connect with prospective clients is through networking events—conferences, association gatherings, workshops, etc. Unfortunately (let's face it), most networking events make us feel awkward. We would rather be anywhere else.

In addition to not knowing anyone, we often feel pressure to hard-sell our services every time someone asks us about our work. Time and again, we suck it up, take a deep breath, and dive in. All in the hope of stirring up some business.

Faced with these pressures, it's natural to experience some fear and discomfort. (Many of my clients feel total dread.) We fear uncomfortable situations in which we're forced to bring in new business in that moment. This angst, however, makes it harder to present ourselves naturally. And when that happens, we don't develop new relationships that might lead to business. Call it a self-fulfilling prophecy—a bad one.

How can we remove the cause of discomfort during networking events?

The key is to change your mindset. Instead of feeling pressured to sell yourself, approach networking with a new perspective. Think of it this way: *Networking has nothing to do with selling.* Rather, networking is about building the right relationships with the right people.

Instead of trying to find clients who will meet *your* needs, think about the people you might be able to help. Focus on those who would be a good fit in your network. As you look for ways to help the people you meet, you will have a greater purpose for being at the event.

One of my clients, a lawyer, went to a networking event and ran into a general counsel from a large company. As they were talking, my client found out that the general counsel's company was about to merge with a larger organization—leading to the loss of his job. My client happened to know of two companies looking for a new general counsel and made introductions. My client's friend did not end up with either job, but the two kept in touch. A few years later, the general counsel worked for a company that was looking for a litigator. That company called my client, which resulted in a $25,000 retainer and a lot of new business.

As you can see, shifting the way you think about networking events will have a direct impact on the way in which you connect with people.

If networking is not about selling, but about getting to know the right people and helping them, then your mindset can switch from *What am I going to get out of this event?* to *Whom can I help at this event?* or *What can I do to support someone else here tonight?* You can also go to the event with excitement and curiosity because you will have the opportunity to meet someone new. By focusing on who you can support, you remove the pressure to sell yourself. That reduces fear. And *that* means that you'll do a better job of presenting yourself.

From a neuroscientific perspective, fear and dread will program your brain to assume the event will be nothing but misery and discomfort. If you program your brain to assume the time will be enjoyable, then you will be predisposed for curiosity and abundance. When you set your brain to wonder, your brain will release dopamine and serotonin. These are feel-good neurochemicals that our bodies produce when we don't feel anxious or threatened. In fact, these chemicals allow us to connect with others on a deeper level. So, being curious and excited about what you might discover and who you might meet at a networking event changes your brain chemistry and outlook.

Our brains and our bodies are directly connected. If your brain says to your body "dread this," then you will personify negativity. Your body language will display fear and discomfort. People will sense those emotions, perhaps leading them to avoid you.

All humans have "mirror neurons." According to Wikipedia's description, mirror neurons are brain cells that mimic or pick up on signals from others around us. They help us feel empathy and to experience the "energy" of social situations. As an example, notice what it is like if you walk into a room where a difficult conversation or a fight has happened. Without anybody saying anything, you can pick up on the negative energy in the room. You might even think that it's pretty "cold in here."

In the same way, if people sense fear, discomfort, or awkwardness in you, they could become uncomfortable, end the conversation, or not even approach you. For this reason, you need remove the natural fear we all experience about networking, change your mindset, and shift the way you present yourself.

Here are a few practical ways to change your mindset. First, remember that *networking is not about selling in that moment*. Networking is only about meeting new people. So, don't go to a networking event with the intent to sell. Instead, go with the intent to meet new people and to build new relationships.

Before you leave for an event or meeting, set yourself up for a successful time. You can do this by playing your favorite music and by taking some centering breaths. You can talk yourself into a state of positivity. For example, you can say to yourself, *I'm curious to see who I will be meeting today*. All of these actions will help you develop a more positive mental framework.

I like to think of this as a pregame warm-up. When we go to the gym, we usually spend about five minutes warming up. Likewise, you can have a warm-up routine before you attend a networking event.

One of my clients likes to play Metallica to get his head in the game. He does this before every event. Once the music starts in his car, he's already gearing up to be social. I have another client who likes to make a deal with herself. She is very uncomfortable meeting strangers, so before every event she decides how many people she will meet (or business cards she wants to collect) and then she only leaves when she hits that number. Sometimes, especially after a long day of talking to people, I will meditate in my car with a five-or-ten-minute meditation on my phone. That helps me get grounded. This is similar to the way professional athletes follow a pregame routine to set themselves up for success. Use whatever method feels right to you. The key is to be deliberate about it.

Some of my next chapters will teach you how to present yourself in a natural and comfortable way so that you won't feel like you're selling yourself. Learning how to do that—to be well-prepared for events—will also increase your confidence and reduce your fears.

Chapter Three

How to Choose the Right Networking Event

Now that you're overcoming the fear of networking events, the next step is to choose the best ones to attend. Keep in mind that networking's sole purpose is to build relationships with new people or to strengthen relationships with those you've connected with in the past.

In my career, which spans more than twenty-five years, I have attended hundreds of networking events. I choose the events I am sincerely interested in. I usually pick the same ones—weekly, monthly, quarterly, and annually. This increases relational continuity and helps me get to know people at a deeper level. Attending a wide array of events sporadically is fine, but it makes it harder to know anyone very well, which results in surface conversations and weak follow-up meetings. Continuity also helps me to learn to speak the "language" of prospective clients. So, I recommend that you consistently attend the same good quality events and get to know some influential people.

If you haven't yet discovered the best networking events, then it is important to invest some time exploring the options. This might mean visiting a whole slew of them until you find the right fit. Where to start? Check out Business Network International (BNI), your local practice association, alumni groups, the Chamber of Commerce, or talk to clients and colleagues who serve on your industry's committees and boards to see which events they attend.

One of my favorite approaches is to talk with a client or prospective client who works within an industry that interests me or might be in my area of expertise. I then ask that person which associations he or she is part of. Quite often you can be brought in as the guest of a long-standing member, which is much easier then showing up cold. Furthermore, your client will likely make complimentary introductions that give you instant credibility.

Best Practices for Attending Conferences

Conferences can be an extremely expensive waste of time. The cost of registration, which can be thousands of dollars, is compounded by time away from work, travel, late nights, and jet lag. It all adds up. Moreover, there typically is no immediate ROI, especially if you don't have a plan before you go. Given the costs involved, make sure you strategically choose the right conferences for your needs and business growth.

Consider the Costs

You should carefully consider your budget for travel, hotel, food, registration, and entertainment. This is true even if you work for a company. It's still worthwhile to do your due diligence to see if the conference is worth your time and the company's resources.

Establish Clear Goals

Beyond the basic costs, there are also strategic factors to consider. It's extremely important to establish goals before you attend a conference. To set a goal and start preparing for a conference, think about why you are going to the conference and what you want to achieve. Are you looking to meet a specific prospect? Are you going to learn something from a speaker you like? Are you going to gather industry information that helps you gain knowledge or expand your services? Your *why* for attending and the goals attached to the *why* are critically important. If you don't have a clear set of goals, then you won't know if the conference you attended was worthwhile or not.

Selecting the Right Conferences for You

After you have identified your goals, the next step is to find the conferences that will most likely help you reach those goals. A good place to start is to ask colleagues, clients, or your association's leaders. These people will give you information about the conferences they attend and which ones are worthwhile in relation to your goals.

I have a good friend who does financial modeling for the Rodeo Association of America. He also does financial modeling for large corporations. His methods are very popular with the rodeo folks. As a result, a large portion of his income is from one rodeo event. Every year, he and his wife attend the National

Finals Rodeo in Las Vegas. This industry event enables him to mix and mingle with his existing clients, the people who appreciate the work he does. Because he attends annually, his business continues to grow. He is a recognized friend in the industry.

The point is this: Relationships generate a lot of opportunity, so it's a good idea to find a conference that fits your purposes and then repeatedly attend the same event. This way you will begin to know the attendees and build your network on a foundation of high-quality relationships. And when you take the time to consider your strategic priorities, you will more likely find a conference that results in those quality relationships—and increased business.

I have a colleague who hopes to break into the global coaching market. That is one of his primary goals. So, he selects industry conferences in Europe where he can meet with professionals in that community. By attending the annual international coaching conferences in Europe, he has established a good reputation and has gained many opportunities for coaching and training in Japan, Spain, and Mexico.

People often overlook another important reason for attending a conference—namely, to learn about professional areas that they know nothing about. Conferences can be a great way to learn about new businesses and market trends. You might discover opportunities that you previously hadn't noticed. Consider attending a conference about a market or profession that is complementary to yours.

For example, if you are an attorney who usually attends legal conferences or CLEs, it might be worthwhile to attend a private equity or accounting conference. If you are an accountant who works with small or mid-size businesses, perhaps consider going to a conference for startups or app developers. The benefits can be tremendous. You can meet new business prospects, new vendors, and find new approaches to your services.

If you have a passion for a hobby or social issue, find a conference that would give you a chance to explore it more from a business perspective. I worked with an attorney who was a partner at a large firm. Her practice mostly consisted of commercial real estate. However, her favorite hobby was adventure travel. After discussing some trips she'd recently taken, I asked her if she had ever thought about attending an adventure travel conference. She hadn't, so we set out to find one. At the conference, she was excited to discover many opportunities for her legal skills in that industry. The exhibitors there were adventure hotels and small businesses that worked with real estate attorneys.

As I mentioned earlier, it's beneficial to attend the same conferences year after year, so as to strengthen and maintain relationships within your network. But you don't want to get tunnel vision. A new perspective can spark your business imagination and help you see opportunities from a completely different paradigm. This paradigm shift might be the catalyst for a new relationship, or a new product, or new service. Doing the same thing for a long time will get stale and can stifle your creative growth.

A few years ago, I took my own advice. As an executive coach and speaker, I typically go to the same events for the International Coach Federation, the Association for Training and Development, and the National Speakers Association. It's great to meet the same people, of course, because I strengthen existing relationships. However, these conferences don't help me meet new people or learn anything astoundingly different. I keep learning variations on the same themes.

So, last year, on a whim, I attended an annual conference for meeting planners, a complementary industry to mine. Meeting planners hire speakers like me, but I wanted to listen to their keynote and breakout speakers, and to connect with vendors at booths to learn what they do and how they do it.

The result was eye opening. I learned what it takes to book a hotel or resort for a large conference, and I learned about industry trends in the convention planning industry. I was particularly interested in how planners are including mindfulness and meditation spaces as a way of serving audiences who are overwhelmed and exhausted from traveling to conferences. I also met a lot of people who work with a speakers' bureau and learned how they look for and book speakers. I even bumped into some clients who go every year to hear the keynote presentations. As a result, I reinforced a relationship and learned how I could better market myself to a specific group and industry, especially around the topic of energy and stress.

The purpose of attending a conference that is related to your industry, or even vastly different, is to open your mind to possibilities and open the door to something that might lead to new business.

In the chart opposite, on one side, make a list of the products and services that you or your firm offers. On the other side, make a list of businesses, services, or products that are complementary to your business. Then look online to see if you can find a conference related to what's listed on the right side of the chart. I would also suggest asking colleagues who work in those complementary areas what conferences they attend, and what they like or dislike about each one.

My products and services	Complementary industries
Architecture	Environmental design

Pre-Conference Preparation

Once you have identified your goals and committed to attend a conference, it's time to put the wheels in motion. I like to prepare a few months before the conference starts. Preparing ahead will help you effectively use your time.

As early as possible, I obtain an attendee list from the conference organizers. They can sometimes be tight-lipped about the current year's list. However, they are usually willing to give you the prior year's guest list. You can use that and an Internet search to gather information from websites about past sponsors and speakers. You can also learn about the awards that were distributed in previous years and get a good feel for who has been attending.

Once you gather all that information, then go to LinkedIn to see if you have any connections with the people or companies that you discovered during your Internet search. If you have a connection, send an email indicating that you will attend the conference and ask if he or she will too. If the person responds, then you can continue the dialogue and even schedule coffee, breakfast, or dinner during the conference. You can at least try to find each other during the networking event, perhaps at a cocktail hour on the first or second day of the event.

Another value in connecting with people prior to the conference is that they can also introduce you to others who will be attending, especially if they have participated before.

If the people you reach via LinkedIn or traditional email say they will not be at the conference, you still have another opportunity to build relationships. Ask them why they've chosen not to go and invite them to meet with you by phone, video conference, or face-to-face at another time. There is no bad time to make or refresh a business relationship.

You can also reach out to the conference speakers. Mention that you are looking forward to hearing them talk and find out if they are speaking at other conferences. Then, when you meet them at the event, you can more easily approach them with a warm introduction instead of a cold one. A phone call before the conference can make it easier to have an in-person conversation.

At the end of the conference, ask the speakers what they thought about the event and which of the conference organizers had hired them. The person who hires speakers is usually an amazing resource because she or he sees industry trends. Knowing people in these positions can be very helpful if you are trying to get a deeper understanding of the market, or if you hope to speak or participate in a panel in the future.

My point is this: Early planning will help you to start building or strengthening relationships with the right people.

Chapter Four

Ditch the Pitch

The Internet has dramatically changed the way people search for and evaluate professional services. Because it is so easy for potential customers to find any service around the globe, we professionals must find a way to build our businesses in more personal ways. The way to avoid being a run-of-the-mill commodity is to build high quality relationships.

The problem is that we often don't do a good job of interacting with people. We don't know how to introduce ourselves or carry on a conversation. As I stated earlier, we struggle because we are stuck in the tired, old-fashioned way of pitching ourselves at networking events.

So, in this chapter I'm going ask you to "ditch the pitch," to throw away the "thirty-second commercial" and develop a better approach to introducing yourself. I'm going to give you a practical strategy for talking to people in a way that opens doors to future business without being pushy or salesy.

What Not to Do

When you attend a networking event, you can be 99 percent sure that someone is going to ask, "What do you do?" How you answer that question will determine whether you have a meaningful and authentic conversation with someone who might be an ideal prospect.

Here's what *not* to do. I'll start with a story. Where I live, there are something like a million business and executive coaches per square inch. One time, while I was at a networking event, someone asked me, "So, what do you do?" I knew that my colleagues and clients responded to this question by giving their titles. So, because I wanted to do some market research, I responded the same way.

"Well," I said, "I'm a coach."

The woman I was talking with rolled her eyes and said, "Goodness! You can't swing a cat in this town without bumping into somebody who calls themselves a coach."

I felt about two-inches tall, as if somebody deflated my "energy balloon." Nevertheless, it was a worthwhile experience. It forced me to think about why it's so hard to make introductions in business environments. I began to think about how to anticipate the ways people respond in these types of conversations.

Some introductions are short but lead to a dead end, such as, "I'm an accountant." It's hard to respond to that statement! Other pitches are thirty seconds of boring that don't give anyone an opening to ask follow-up questions. When I hear a thirty-second textbook spiel, I need someone to pinch me to wake me up.

Standard approaches don't work. Networking events are supposed to be opportunities to have real conversations. If *we* are bored with what we are saying, it only makes sense that *others* will be bored too. In fact, at the end of the networking event I described above, I realized that I hadn't generated any meaningful connections. The people I met weren't that interested in me, and I also wasn't too interested in talking to them. But I did learn one thing: Answering the question, "What do you do?" in a blunt and boring way will dramatically reduce the chances of developing an interesting conversation that can lead to future meetings. It's what I call "conversation buzzkill."

So, what *should* you do?

What You Should Do

The strategy for short networking conversations with new contacts is simple. First, do your research before the event so you have some idea about who will be there. Then try to find the right people, perhaps from your Internet search, or perhaps by conversing with people you meet at the event. Forget the sales pitch. Just start conversing.

Second, try to help the people you meet gain a natural interest in what you do. Hopefully they will have enough interest to be an organic part of your relational network, people whom you can help and who could open opportunities in the future for you. Remember, it takes time to get new business.

How to Introduce Yourself

The best way to introduce yourself is to first think about what you like to do and why you are in your business. Also, you should be prepared to explain what you are working on—your projects—in a way that might generate interest among those you meet.

Take time to think about and write down some creative ways to share these aspects of your work and yourself—without a sales pitch! You want people to understand *what* you do (not just your title) and *why* you do it (your passions and motivations).

Before you attend a networking event, you should also think about the types of people you will be meeting. Then modify your introduction accordingly. Tailor your questions and personal introduction to the event that you will be attending or, if possible, to the people you would most like to meet. Do what you can beforehand to make your conversations relevant and meaningful.

For example, as an executive coach and business strategist, I work with a lot of professionals in law, accounting, private equity, etc. When I'm at a conference filled with lawyers, I say that I help lawyers understand how to manage their time to avoid burnout without sacrificing revenue. And if I'm attending an event where there are a lot of CEOs and representatives of Fortune 500 companies, I tailor my introduction this way: "Hi, my name is Stephanie. I'm an executive coach who does a lot of work on leadership and communication, especially with executives who manage large teams." If that generates curiosity, I tell them what I've learned about trust as the foundation for team development. I'll express my passion for working with those types of teams.

That's all I will say. I'm clear about what I do, who I do it for and with, and what is happening in the broader market. My work involves a lot more than communication and time management, but a networking introduction is not the time to download everything I do. That conversation usually happens when I set up a follow-up meeting.

The Introduction without the Pitch

The purpose of the introduction is not to sell yourself; it is simply to *leave the window open* for a conversation based on what you share about yourself.

Due to the shortening of our attention spans, you have about fifteen seconds to authentically generate interest in what you do. You hope that people will ask you a follow-up question that sets the stage for a deeper and more meaningful conversation. You want to showcase who you are and what you do in a natural, authentic, and meaningful way. The preparation you (hopefully) do before the event is critical to making this happen.

Today's fifteen-second attention span has an upside. It should force us to avoid sharing every detail about ourselves. I've often met people at networking events who give me a menu of what they do. Most people really don't care about all the ins and outs of your work when you first meet them. The fifteen-second limit will help you stay focused on what's most compelling. If the other person asks for more information, you can share something related to what he or she asks. Again, an introduction is only about starting a conversation, not about sharing our resumes in the hopes of immediately getting new business.

Here are some good examples of introductions when someone asks, "What do you do?"

Example: "Hi, I'm Stephanie. I have an executive coaching and training company. I help a lot of busy people manage their time and energy so that they can be more productive and less stressed."

Example: "My name is John. I'm a real estate lawyer with XYZ company and I'm having a lot of fun these days looking at all the new commercial development in downtown Denver, especially with the new green spaces that are being built on roofs."

Example: "Hi, my name is Josh. I'm an accountant with my own practice. I really enjoy helping businesses understand all the new tax regulations. I like giving business leaders clarity as we go through a lot of change."

Example: "Hi, my name is Greg. I do outside

general counsel work. These days I'm very busy helping HR departments and companies face challenges of managing social media and preventing cyber theft."

These types of simple introductions will give the person you're speaking with a basic idea about your work in a way that opens a window for more dialogue. And there is no selling involved!

After the Intro, What Next?

After you have made your introduction and heard a little about the person you have just met, you can surmise whether he or she is interested in knowing more about you or whether you are interested in getting to know him or her more. If neither is the case, then usually the conversation will naturally come to an end. But if there is mutual interest, you need to make sure that you ask some excellent follow-up questions. Your questions should be connected to something the other person has revealed about himself or herself. So, make sure that you are an attentive listener.

I highly recommend that you don't extend the dialogue for too long. Nobody likes to talk to one person endlessly at a networking event when everyone is trying to move around the room. If you'd like to get to know the person more, ask if she or he would like to continue the conversation over coffee or on a phone call in the near future. If the answer is yes, then ask for the person's business card and tell her or him that you will send an email with some possible dates and times. Leave it at that, but make sure to follow up—otherwise it's a lost opportunity.

Chapter Five

Simple Strategies for Success at Networking Events

There are many intricacies involved in relating to people at networking events. For example, how should you end a conversation if someone is clinging to you? How should you break into a huddled group? Where should you put your name tag? In this chapter, I will give you some proven strategies to help you get the most out of an event and leave with a feeling of accomplishment rather than defeat.

Bring a Wingman or Wingwoman

Going to a networking event with a colleague, friend, or associate will help you feel more comfortable. Just be careful to not be overdependent on the friend or colleague who attends with you. The key to making the event successful, of course, is to meet new people. So, avoid the temptation to only hang out with your friend in a personal comfort zone.

You might be with a colleague who, due to personal insecurities, sticks to you more than you would like. I once went to a networking event with a business colleague who was next to me literally every time I turned my head. I felt like a mom with a four-year old who wouldn't leave my side.

I got around this situation by connecting my colleague with another person. When I met the next person and introduced myself, I also introduced my friend and said, "I'll leave the two of you to talk." Then I took off to meet someone new. It doesn't have to be harsh, just effective.

Prepare Questions in Advance

At the beginning of each event day, think about the questions you'd like to ask the people you meet. This will prevent you from fumbling in your first conversations or during your one-to-one meetings. I, for one, can't stand it when people ask, "So, what do you do?" I suppose that's necessary, but you should try to ask questions that generate interesting conversations. Networking is about getting to know people in order to determine if you'd like to know them more. It's better to ask, "What made you decide on this networking group?" or, "How does this networking group align with the work you do?" or "What is happening in your work that really interests you these days?" These types of questions give people a comfortable opportunity to share more about themselves. Good questions will help you develop natural relationships.

Politely Interrupt

People often ask me, "Is it okay to interrupt a group conversation to introduce myself?" The answer is absolutely yes. Everyone at networking events is there to meet new people. So, there is no problem with stepping into a group and politely introducing yourself. The rest typically takes care of itself.

Overcoming Introversion

So, you're an introvert. What now? It's challenging for introverted people to network. It can drain your battery. The way around that is to give yourself a goal. For example, you might set a goal to meet five new people. Push yourself to meet that goal and then you can head back home.

You can also bribe yourself. Let's say you meet your goal of meeting five good business contacts. Reward yourself with an ice cream (or something less fattening). Introverts can do the same amount of networking as extroverts; however, it is more draining for introverts. Therefore, having a plan for how to replenish a depleted social battery will help immensely.

Follow Up

I will address this topic more thoroughly later in the book, but let me emphasize now the importance of following up with people within one-to-three days after an event. Sending an email is fine. If you'd like to set up a coffee or lunch meeting, you can put that into your email. Also set up a CRM or a spreadsheet and include the following information: names, basic details about their interests, which event you met them at, and your follow-up plan. You'll find an outline of an excel CRM that I use on my website (stephaniewachman.com) under resources. As part of your follow-up plan, it's important to also connect on LinkedIn within one-to-three days after an event.

How to Handle One-to-One Meetings

Hopefully you were able to schedule one-to-one meetings in advance. But how can you effectively use those meetings during a networking event? Be sure to enter the meeting with the right mentality. Look for ways to help people rather than pursuing your own interests. In addition to learning about the other event participants, try to find out who they know and who they might be able to connect you with. You can do the same for them by offering the contact information of people who might be helpful to them. Finally, don't let the meeting end without suggesting a follow-up discussion at a later date. Tell them you hope to stay in touch over the long-term.

Chapter Six

Strengthen Relationships after Networking Events

Now that you've spent a lot of time, money, and emotional energy attending a networking event, it would be a huge mistake to not follow up with some of the people with whom you've connected.

It's best to contact people within a couple of weeks after the event. This does not mean taking every business card you've collected and sending "nice to meet you" emails to every person. You should be deliberate and selective about who you choose to contact. So, now it's time to do your homework.

If you met a few interesting people at the event, look them up on LinkedIn and with an Internet search. Discover more about their organizations and who they are connected to; then decide if you would like to schedule follow-up meetings with them.

As you do this basic research, you might find that the people you met are professionals in the same market as you. However, that doesn't mean they are competitors. Some of them could be your allies. They might be excellent resources, if for no other reason than as a source of referrals.

Mindset: Think about Giving, not Taking

Remember that your goal is to potentially help them! We get so caught up in finding work for ourselves that networking can become selfish. My view is very different.

I frequently meet with people who could be considered competitors, but I have learned that we can be amazing allies. They have helped me collaborate on bigger projects that I couldn't handle on my own. Likewise, I have helped colleagues make thousands of dollars because they were able to add value to my clients in ways that I couldn't.

A few years ago, I met an HR consultant at a networking event and we chatted over coffee. A few months later she introduced me to a large private equity firm whose executives hoped to find a coach for one of the company's analysts. That opportunity led to more coaching and the launch of a women's leadership program. A few years later, a company leader asked if I would be interested in bidding on a global corporate culture initiative. The firm wanted to improve its overall employee experience at all of its offices around the world. The company had experienced large growth, but the small-firm culture that had worked in the beginning wasn't keeping up. As a result, there were many different offices operating like individual entities rather than as one unified company.

I had never done anything on this scale, but I knew someone who had. I reached out to a colleague (and competitor) and asked if he'd be interested in working with me on this opportunity. He agreed. We went to bat against the likes of McKinsey & Co., and we won the business, which resulted in a lucrative two-year engagement.

Later, this same "competitor" recommended me to one of his major clients. I provided executive coaching and worked with him on overflow.

The bottom line is this: You should not think about networking only through the lens of what's in it for you. You should consider ways to help the people in your network. Pay close attention to those you want in your network and build those relationships. Unimaginable opportunities can appear.

How to Connect

Now that you have done your research about a few people, and assuming that you wish to develop several relationships, you should connect with those prospects on LinkedIn and send an email stating that you enjoyed meeting them at the event. Tell them you would like to meet with them and suggest a few dates and times.

This is what I typically say: "Hi Jim. It was great meeting you last night at the chamber meeting. I would enjoy grabbing coffee with you in the next few weeks and learning more about what you do. How does Monday or Thursday of next week look for you? If those dates don't work, let me know of a better day and time. I look forward to hearing from you soon."

It's that simple.

Prepare for the Meeting

Your contact has agreed to meet you. The date, time, and place has been set. What next?

Never show up to a meeting unprepared, or it will be a total waste of time and energy for you and the other person. Most professional service providers bill by the hour or even by the minute, so it's critical to use your time well. That doesn't mean spending hours doing research. It only takes fifteen or twenty minutes.

Preparation starts by accessing LinkedIn and an Internet search engine to learn about the person with whom you will be meeting. When reviewing the profile, look for commonalities about the person's company that seem relevant to you. Learn some basic information about the firm. I also recommend setting up news alerts about the person or company so that you can stay current. I find it helpful to take a screen shot of the person's profile and include his or her picture. This way you won't have to wander awkwardly around the coffee shop looking for the person when you arrive for the meeting. I've seen a lot of business people in coffee shops struggling to find the right person. It's embarrassing to watch as they go from table to table asking, "Are you Janet?"

Think about what questions to ask during the meeting. These questions should display a genuine interest in the person, and they should also be connected to your goals for the meeting. Some questions to consider:

- What brought you to your company?
- Why did you choose this company?

- How did you settle on this area of expertise?
- Your LinkedIn profile shows that you went to XYZ university. What made you choose that school?
- What trends are you seeing in the market and what are some of your biggest challenges?
- Outside of work, what do you like to do for fun?
- What brought you to where you live now? (Whenever someone asks me that question, it opens up a great conversation. I moved to Denver from my home in Montreal after meeting my husband on an online dating site in the 1990s, back when online dating was still dial-up. We've been married for over twenty years now and we have a beautiful family. As you can see, some questions can lead to all kinds of fun information.)
- Do you attend any other networking events? What are your favorite conferences?

Once you've built a comfortable rapport, then you can dive into business questions, such as: What brought you to XYZ company? What do you enjoy most about your work? What are some of your long-term goals for your business? You should ask open-ended questions, allowing for deeper conversation.

I have already discussed the importance of helping other people. During your meetings with new contacts, or even when revisiting old ones, you might see specific ways to help them. If during the meeting you discover you like the person, and if she or he has a significant network, then I recommend sharing your ideas for helping them. You can do this easily by asking if the person is interested in meeting someone in *your* network. This is a very natural approach, one that is far better than asking, "How can I help you?" That sounds contrived, it is too open-ended, and everyone knows it's formulaic.

In summary, make sure that you are prepared. Have clear goals, good questions, and an awareness of how you might be able to help the other person. Then if you establish an initial connection, be sure to follow up. Close the loop on your commitments. Doing so will show your reliability and your character.

How to Start the Conversation

Starting a meeting conversation the right way will help the dialogue flow and set the tone for a natural connection. Here's a story about the *wrong way*.

I was scheduled to meet a marketing strategist on Zoom (a video conferencing app) who wanted to pitch me an online product-launch program. As soon as the Zoom camera came on, and before I even got in a "hello," he said, "Do you want me to tell you about all the things I've done?"

I was taken aback. I always like to "date" first before I jump into a "serious relationship." So, I said, "How about we start with hello?"

He smiled, shook his head, and said, "Yes, of course. I'm sorry. I stink at small talk."

Many of us may think small talk is a waste of time, but it is a key component of building relationships and trust.

People are hardwired to connect. Even though we are not conscious of it, the circuitry in our brains since the beginning of time has been designed to be social. The need to be part of a community and to belong is incredibly powerful. Not only does social connection make us feel good, it decreases our levels of cortisol and adrenalin—the neuro chemicals that are present when we are uncomfortable or under a lot of stress. By contrast, when connecting in healthy ways with other people, we produce oxytocin, dopamine, and serotonin—the neuro chemicals that promote bonding and enable us to think bigger, think more broadly, and feel appreciation. Stress causes the opposite to happen. We think about short-term survival—fight or flight. So, connecting with others and building relationships is vital to business development. All of this should give you a positive mindset as you enter the meeting. You should enjoy it!

I took a certification course in conversation and neuroscience. I wanted to learn how the brain is designed to connect. Titled "Conversational Intelligence," the course was taught by the late Judith Glaser. In the class, she had us do an exercise called, "What's in a name?" In this exercise, we all asked each other how we got our names. It's amazing how much you can learn about a person by asking that question. It's also amazing how comfortable people feel when they share about that topic. I spoke about getting my name from my grandmother, who was born in Russia. I shared her story about landing as an immigrant in Canada after losing family members to the plague. This small bit of information opened up a broad and interesting conversation. When the class debriefed at the end of the exercise, we were asked to write down how we *felt*. Everyone wrote the same descriptive words: connected, comfortable, happy.

Discussing feelings with businesspeople in my training sessions or as a speaker is usually a way for me to quickly lose my audience. But because humans are wired for connection, we need to be authentic, to use our natural personalities to enrich our businesses and our lives.

It is possible, as you can see, to make your initial meetings with people enjoyable, especially in the first minutes of the meeting. The barrier that I see frequently is urgency, the urgency to build a relationship that isn't based on authentic connection, or that is based *only* on the selfish intent of getting business.

When we feel pressure to sell ourselves all the time, meeting people becomes a huge turnoff for us and for others. So, change your thinking. Building relationships is not about selling; it's about connecting with the right people who have a good network, the people you can help and who can help you.

You don't have to ask the people you meet how they got their names; a different approach is fine. But remember that the purpose of a first conversation is to learn about people and what they do, and to discover if they are a good fit for your network and vice versa. To emphasize my earlier point, your pre-meeting preparation is the key to a successful encounter. Preparing good questions that allow people to open up is the foundation for building strong and trusting relationships. If you keep that in mind, you will reduce stress and increase your authenticity. Business opportunities will be the natural outgrowth of your real relationships—and you won't have to do a hard sell.

Chapter Seven

Old Selling vs. New Selling

Building a network of potential clients occurs best when we focus on authentic interactions rather than feeling pressured to constantly pitch ourselves. However, we still need to line up real business and generate revenue. How can we encourage the people we connect with to come on board as paying clients, but without the sales pitch?

The traditional model of selling forces us to meet as many prospects as possible, pitch ourselves, get an appointment, and then try hard to close the deal. This is an old framework that needs to be abolished, especially within the professional services sector. In order to see the difference between the traditional style of sales and the approach I recommend, we need to look closely at the reasons why the traditional method is inadequate.

Old-school selling, about which there are millions of books and training programs, is about identifying the customer's major "pain points." To do this, the method requires us to ask questions such as: "What is troubling you about the services that you currently have? Does your current consultant *really* listen to you?" Then, if the customer reveals some pain, we pounce. "Oh, your consultant doesn't listen to you? Wow! It must be really hard to be ignored. Let me tell you about how *our* firm does it differently."

Picking at pain points is like someone who constantly pokes you; it's totally annoying. Most prospects are well-attuned to that model . . . because so many salespeople use it! The pain-points model has poked and pressured so many of us that we are already annoyed before we get going.

The old-school sales model says we should meet people at networking events and immediately start pitching our products and services, even if the people we meet never ask us about our products and services. This is completely impersonal.

I'll give you an example. I was recently with my son while he was trying a new judo club for the first time. At the end of the session, the owner said, "Hey, let me give you a judo uniform. It's $56 and here you go." She aggressively threw the uniform at me to catch without even asking my son if he enjoyed the class or wanted to continue. She never asked if we had any questions. She was just selling me stuff without showing any care, concern, or curiosity about our needs. She just said, "Here, buy this." I felt very uncomfortable.

That's what it feels like when you pitch your products and services without having any authentic concern for your prospect or customer. That's why old-school sales methods don't work well. So, avoid the hard sell. Only talk about your products and services after you've sought to genuinely understand your client's or prospect's needs, and only when people request information. Otherwise, you're just going to bombard them with information that they don't need or want. And no one wants to be bombarded. They'll run for safety.

The old-school method of sales even shows up in email exchanges. I once met a woman at a networking event who was a life coach, chiropractor, and a healing energy practitioner . . . and a hairstylist. At the event, she started pushing me to sign up for a consultation. (I'm still not clear which of her services she talked about.) After a lot of pressure, she finally cornered me. I was trapped with nowhere to go. So, to escape the situation, I said, "Okay, just send me some information and we'll see what happens."

I got an email from her a couple of weeks later. I'd like you to read this email because it's an example of what you should never do.

Hi, Stephanie. We met at the Chamber Business Meeting a few weeks ago. I hope your speaking presentation went well. Unfortunately, I was not able to attend that morning. I'm a life coach and energy healing practitioner, and I'm a hairstylist as well. I'm reaching out to you to see if you'd like to meet with me and know more about the services I offer. We have spoken before about energy healing sessions. [She was the only one talking, I might add.] I'm offering them at night so people can go straight to bed after them and continue to rejuvenate (smiley face). Would you be interested to meet with me and see how we can support each other? I'd love to support and serve you in any way I can. I'm looking forward to hearing from you.

There's so much wrong with this email. I don't even know where to begin. She's making a lot of assumptions. She seems to think we had a long conversation about healing, which we certainly did not. We only talked for about thirty seconds at the Chamber event, because she was talking *at* me. She never asked me if I *needed* any kind of healing. I sleep just fine at night, so I don't know why I would need to go straight to bed and continue to rejuvenate. I don't have those issues. She making all these assumptions and pushing her services on me. The tone of this email turned me off, so I just hit delete.

There is a better way. Her email could have been something like this: "Hey, we met at the Chamber event a couple of weeks ago. I'm really curious to learn more about the work that you do as an executive coach. I was wondering how you support your clients with energy and time management. I'm also in that field and I think we might have a lot in common. Why don't we sit down and talk?"

Now, that would have been a much more engaging approach for me. I would have thought, *Oh, this is interesting. She actually gets what I do, and I could learn more about what she does, and maybe we could refer people to each other.* But her old-school selling method pushed me away. This story demonstrates why it's important to be deliberate and thoughtful about how you approach people.

The How and When of Offering Proposals

It's also a mistake to assume that everybody wants a proposal from you. When I worked in business development for a prominent uniform organization, we would use cold calls as our sales approach. We would make a call and say, "Hey, it looks like your contract with XYZ company is coming up. Can I drop off a proposal from our company so that you can compare it with what you have now?"

That approach doesn't usually result in new business. Why? Because no effort is given to building relationships. Not only that, this method forces the sales staff to spend a lot of time putting proposals together for people who don't even want them. There is no mutuality in this approach.

It would be more authentic and relational to say, "Tell me a little bit more about what you're looking for. I would like to know how I might support you." Then, after you have listened, you might ask a follow-up question like this: "If I put a proposal together, would you be interested in having a conversation about it before we get into fees, costs, and pricing?" In other words, you should have a dialogue. A relational approach is more likely to lead to referrals and new business.

In all of your interactions, be careful to choose wording that builds connection and trust. Avoid salesy words and employ language that is authentic and personal. Instead of pushing a sales pitch at the end of a meeting, say something like this: "What do we want to do with this?" or, "How do you see this service fitting into your company?" Leave the ball in the other person's court but make yourself available to help. You can ask questions such as: "What do you want to do next?" or, "How can we help you?" or, "Are there any other services you would like to know about?" or, "Let me know if you'd like to see a proposal on what we discussed."

In summary, old-school selling prevents you from being authentic to who you are. It forces you to be salesy, to follow an impersonal formula. This makes you and prospective clients feel uncomfortable.

Put Your Clients First

There is a better way. You can effectively sell your products and services while also being real and personal. I call it "client-focused sales." By this I mean that your primary goal is to produce the best outcome possible *for your prospects and clients*. When we focus on what our prospects need, we will find ways to authentically help them. By contrast, if you're only interested in selling your widget to bolster your own bottom line, then you're not client-focused. Rather, you are self-focused. If you think about what the widget can do to solve your clients' problems or to improve their businesses, then you're thinking about *their* outcomes as opposed to *your* outcomes. That's a very important distinction. It's a different mindset. Think about the value you bring to each engagement.

As I previously mentioned, most clients and prospects can easily learn about products and services online. Therefore, we should sincerely strive to educate them at a broader level. We can inform them about industry trends that they probably don't know about. That honest effort to help them learn, which puts them first, can give you a competitive edge. It sets you apart as a caring and knowledgeable visionary in the context of your field.

If you're in professional services, you might talk about how technology is impacting the industry. If you're an accountant, you can share about new accounting regulations. If you're a lawyer, you can educate your clients about how new legislation might impact their businesses. If you're selling products, you can talk about what you're learning in relation to product development, recycling, or environmental work. Whatever it is, find a way to provide valuable information that your clients can't find online.

Importantly, this relational approach will help *you* feel more comfortable in your sales efforts. It's very important to work from a place of true self as opposed forcing yourself into a formula that you learned during a sales training course.

I strongly encourage you to approach sales opportunities authentically and naturally. Prepare ahead of time so that you're not stumbling over your words and trying to figure out what to do next. Instead of pushing stuff on people, always focus on how much value you can bring to each engagement.

Chapter Eight

Speak! (To Gain More Business)

A fantastic way to gain exposure and build credibility in a natural way is by speaking at events and conferences. If you are comfortable speaking to large or small groups, think about building these types of engagements into your business plan. If speaking makes you shudder but you really want to try it, then there are some steps you can take to overcome your fears and improve your ability.

This chapter is not about public speaking techniques or how to become a professional speaker. Rather, I'm presenting a methodology for how to attract new business by speaking to groups. If you would like to learn more about public speaking skills, I encourage you to join a Toastmasters group or connect with a local chapter of the National Speakers Association. These two organizations offer terrific opportunities for experienced and aspiring speakers to practice the art of speaking and become more comfortable doing it.

The Benefits of Speaking

A few years ago, I spoke at the Colorado Legal Inclusiveness Association (CLI). Following my talk, I was asked by two different law firms to speak to their attorneys. I had spoken for free at the associations. As a result, I was hired to speak at a number of firms for my regular fee.

Speaking, and the exposure it brings, is also one of the easiest ways to build up your contacts for your newsletter or blog. There are a number of ways to do that. The first is to ask people in the audience to fill out an evaluation form. (You can download a model from the resources page on my website.) On the form, ask for feedback about your talk. Try to find out what worked, what would make it better, and what were the greatest takeaways. Also ask people if they would like to be added to your newsletter, or if they would like you to contact them for further conversation about the topic. This gives you valuable feedback and gives you permission to stay in touch with them, either through your newsletter or email.

How to Get Started As a Speaker

If you are just starting out as a speaker, a good approach is to find local associations that might be interested in your topic. For example, if you want to develop new clients in a specific tech industry, you can contact a tech start-up association or a trade association that represents that industry.

Another way to begin is by sitting on a panel with other experts, or by moderating a panel. Many networking events in your city have a need for speakers. These opportunities are typically not paid gigs, but they can help you bolster your speaking resume and build a "portfolio" so that you can take your speaking opportunities to a higher level.

Keep in mind that many people who come to hear you speak might also need your services; so, in addition to improving your speaking skills, you will have natural opportunities to connect with people who might not have known about you. Some of them might want to work with you.

How to Pick a Topic

Hot topics will generate the most interest and momentum. A good way to pick a hot topic is with an online search. Use keywords related to your topic to see how many search results come up for it. If you can take that information and put a spin on it to make it your own, then you are golden.

If you are in a profession that must constantly work around new legislation or tax codes, then you can speak on legislative trends and how they will affect your audience's businesses or personal lives. I have a client who specializes in cybersecurity law. When bitcoin became more popular, my client spoke to numerous groups to help them understand bitcoin and how it could impact security. This was (and is) a very relevant and hot topic.

Another great way to find a hot topic is to ask your clients about their interests. This will improve your relationships with existing clients and give you real-time feedback on their needs. That's a great way to develop relationships, perhaps opening opportunities to follow-up with them.

Invite Your Clients

When I first started speaking, I made the big mistake of not inviting my clients to the conference or association meetings where I spoke. As an unpaid or paid speaker, you are generally allowed to bring some friends to the event for free. Take the organizers up on the offer and invite as many of your clients and prospects as you can, especially if they helped you in some way.

Steps for Finding Opportunities and Ideas

Here is a step-by-step guide that will help ensure that you don't miss any opportunities when planning a speaking event.

Step 1: Identify association events and conferences where your topic would be of interest.

Step 2: Ask your existing clients what associations and events they participate in and if they can introduce you to any of the members.

Step 3: Work on your topic. See what you can find through online searches and then see if you can put your own twist on the topic. For example, when I speak on time management, my spin is related to my first book, *Own Your Time*. My book and presentation are about more than just scheduling. They address the specific needs of my clients, one of which is stress—a hot topic!

Step 4: Write a short description about the talk

and explain what the participants will gain from it. This is very important. Who wants to go to a talk and not know what they will gain from it? My advice is to keep your description short. Most people don't have the attention span to read a long essay. It's best to be concise. Reach out to prospects and clients and ask them to give you feedback on the *description* of your presentation. Then invite them to hear you speak at the event. (If they decline, let them know that you will be following up to share how it went.)

Step 5: Put your talk together and start practicing. Don't stop practicing until it's time to deliver the presentation. Make sure your timing and content is right. A dry run is always a good idea. Sometimes I gather people from my network and offer them a "free presentation" in exchange for feedback. Most libraries don't charge for meeting rooms, so it won't cost you anything and the feedback is incredibly valuable. Use the evaluation form and don't be reluctant to ask questions about what you could have done better. You will get tons of valuable ideas for improvement.

Step 6: Before you speak, ask the event organizers if they can introduce you to a few association members so that you can learn about the industry and its lingo. This will strengthen your relationships with the audience members and give you confidence that you are on the right track. By making connections with some of them before the event, the audience won't feel as "cold" to you when you speak.

Step 7: Let your social media network know that you are doing a presentation and give them the details. I suggest using LinkedIn. If you work for a firm that has a newsletter and blog, use that platform to communicate your message.

Step 8: Always show up early on the day of the presentation. This will reduce stress, give you time for final preparations, and enable you to see the venue.

Step 9: Hang around after the presentation so that the audience has a chance to speak with you one-to-one. It's in those moments that people exchange business cards and possibly schedule follow-up meetings. If you are invited to a networking cocktail hour or lunch before or after your talk, it should be your "best practice" to attend. More people will have an opportunity to talk to you, and you might find some prospective clients.

Step 10: If someone after your presentation says she or he would like to talk more, then you should schedule a time right away. Say, "I'm so pleased that you liked my presentation. I'd like to learn more about your business and situation. Let's set a time to talk before I leave." If that isn't possible, ask, "What if I send you a few dates for when we could talk and then you can look at your schedule?" In other words, don't let the fish off the hook. Act quickly because as soon as they leave the event, the real world will come flooding in.

Step 11: Follow up. If you said you would send a document or article, then make sure to keep your word. If a prospect or client helped you with topic ideas, then call or send a thank you card. A little show of gratitude goes a long way.

Step 12: Ask yourself what worked, what didn't, and what you would do differently the next time. Debriefing yourself is a way to grow and develop, but do it without being too harsh on yourself.

Step 13: Now that you have your talk "in the can" (so to speak), find more opportunities to share your message.

Speaking is one of the best ways to stir up new business. As I mentioned earlier, you can hone your speaking skills by joining a group like Toastmasters, or even an improvisation group, to get more comfortable on stage. Take a few risks, test yourself, and see how you like it.

Chapter Nine

Growing and Sustaining Your Business

A recent study found that 44 percent of professionals gave up on a new prospect after only one follow-up attempt. That's discouraging, especially when you realize that 80 percent of sales occur after at least five follow-up connections.

This chapter is about maintaining a consistent presence in your networks and about developing a mechanism by which you can stay in touch with the network you have worked so hard to develop— especially with prospects who fit your ideal customer profile. Being relational over the long-term will make it much easier to grow your business.

There are basically three types of people in your network: new prospects and recent clients; dormant clients; and referral sources. I have divided this chapter to address each of the three.

Following Up with New Prospects

We've discussed how to reach out in relational ways to new prospects in earlier chapters. Here, I want to encourage you to *follow up* with the people you meet at networking events or conferences. You should do this within one-to-three days after a meeting.

If after the first follow-up attempt you haven't seen much response, don't give up (see the statistics above). Sometimes a slow response is not related to disinterest in you. People are busy. They forget. So, persist a few more times while maintaining your authentic relational approach (no selling!). Once you've made the first outreach attempt, the next step is to create a system whereby you are consistently connecting and reconnecting. On my website, you will find some templates for what to say in your follow-up attempts with new prospects.

Dormant Clients: The Low Hanging Fruit

Dormant clients are people who have worked with you in the past, people who like you, and (equally important) people you like. These clients may have finished a project with you and then disappeared from your radar.

Dormant clients are important. You might only need to trigger their memory to ramp up new business with them. Some of them may have switched jobs or companies. If so, this gives you a natural reason to reconnect. When you reach out, they often realize that they need your services but hadn't had a chance to call you.

I addressed the topic of calling on dormant clients while speaking at a law conference. I saw one accountant's eyes light up. She blurted out, "Oh my gosh! I haven't reached out to one of my clients in a long time." At the break, she made a quick call to the dormant client who said, "Oh, your timing is perfect. We really need your services." This proved to be a huge opportunity. That one call brought in $30,000 worth of new business. I have witnessed many other examples like that one.

Contacting your happy past clients also helps you avoid cold calling, which is terribly uncomfortable for most of us. Even if they don't need your services at the moment, re-engaging with them is a natural and relational way to keep you top-of-mind.

Look for a natural reason to call your dormant clients. My favorite is to ask for feedback. By asking a dormant (or existing) client for feedback, you naturally remind him or her of your previous work. As you reconnect, the client might share a new problem, enabling you to offer a solution. The feedback can serve as great testimonial content for your website that helps to differentiate you from competitors. Ask him or her how you or your firm's services have helped, how he or she would describe what you do, and how you can improve.

I once called a dormant client after reading that he had made it into the top rankings of lawyers in *Colorado* magazine. I reached out to congratulate him. In this situation, I thought a phone call would be more personal than email. I knew he would know my name when he saw my number on his phone. When he answered, I said, "How's it going? Congratulations on achieving this massive goal of being recognized as one of the best lawyers in Colorado." He was really excited to hear from me.

He also let slip a clue when he said, "It's great, but I'm freaking out because I heard from another lawyer that when you get this kind of recognition, you get a million phone calls and opportunities from prospective clients." In theory, this is a great problem to have; but when you are a solo practitioner, it can be overwhelming to accept new opportunities without disappointing existing clients. As your business grows, your capacity shrinks.

So, I asked a follow-up question. "Tell me, how are you going to plan for the growth that you're going to see?" He paused and said, "Oh, I'd better sit down with you and work on this."

There you have it. A sincere desire to congratulate a former client naturally opened a new opportunity. My objective was to congratulate and reconnect, and he was happy to hear from me. The next steps came naturally for both of us. There was no "selling" involved, just open-ended questions and authentic friendship; and that led to more business.

These examples demonstrate why calling on dormant clients is a great way to generate revenue and to help your clients.

Here's an important tip: If your business is a little slow between projects, that's a good time to follow up with your dormant clients. Make a good effort to sustain your network as a part of your "sales without being salesy" habit. Go through your list of former clients and call on a few each week. Set up LinkedIn or Google to notify you if there are any events that might present a natural opportunity to contact those people again.

How to Follow Up with Referral Sources

Referral sources are people who have referred your services to others. They may have used your services in the past, or perhaps not, but it's important to stay connected with them. They are a great source for finding new opportunities.

Statistics show that a person needs to follow up with a prospect at least nine times before they will get any new business. But most of us give up after two attempts because we don't want to feel like stalkers. If we would make a few more attempts over the course of several months, then we might win some new business.

I do a lot of work in the professional services industries with lawyers, accountants, and private equity experts. At a networking event, I met a woman who owns a career placement company. I really enjoyed our conversation and followed up with her the next day. Over lunch we talked about our businesses and I asked her how I could help her. She did the same thing with me. A few weeks later, she called to ask if I would be interested in speaking with one of her past clients who was seeking an executive coach. She referred me because I was top-of-mind and fit the person's criteria. It turned out to be a great opportunity. I worked with her client for six months and we had an excellent engagement.

This example demonstrates how a connection can become a referral source. Because we developed a good relationship, I have sent her referrals and she has sent referrals to me as the need comes up. We make it a point to have lunch once per quarter to keep in touch.

Sometimes you can ask a dormant client for referrals. The way to do that naturally is to say, "Could you make an introduction for me?" It's as simple as that because you have already developed a strong relationship with your dormant client. It's not that hard to ask for an introduction.

You should keep referral sources on a follow-up schedule so that it's not one and done. Being deliberate and having a plan about how you are going to invest in those relationships is critical.

When creating a follow-up schedule, build a list of all your referral sources and potential referral sources. Write down why you are reaching out to them and what you want to say. Develop a short strategy for every meeting that you have. Don't just show up at meetings without having a clear plan and goals.

I'd like to make one last point about referral sources: Try to develop relationships with referral sources and dormant clients who have large networks in your area of expertise. These people have a wider array of connections, which often makes them the best sources for referrals.

In summary, following up consistently will generate revenue for your business. We miss opportunities when we aren't paying attention to our existing and past business connections. Finding the right peer partners and referral sources is a great way to grow your business through relationships. You don't have to sell anything. You just have to be yourself, be relational, and look for ways to help others.

Leveraging Existing Clients for More Opportunities

Most of us have ideal clients with whom we are working and enjoying strong relationships. These client relationships often go on "cruise control." We simply maintain them. We forget to pay attention to opportunities and important changes in the lives of the people we know.

These changes often occur within one organization. If your contact person happens to leave the organization, you might not have any more access to that company. For this reason, it is important to develop relationships on multiple levels within each organization. When you only know one person within a company, your situation becomes more tenuous.

One of my clients had been providing legal services to a manufacturing company for over five years. Unfortunately, the only relationship he had was with the general counsel. When the organization was acquired by a private equity company, the new directors replaced the entire leadership team and the president. Everything changed rapidly.

The incoming president had a best friend who was a lawyer, a lawyer he had met during his university years and with whom he had worked for many years. Slowly but surely, my client got squeezed out—even though he had proven himself to be a trusted advisor and even though his prices were more competitive. It all boiled down to the relationship the president had with his friend. Because my client only had a connection with the general counsel, he no longer had anyone who could advocate for him and the value of his service to the company.

Think about your best clients. Do you have connections with multiple leaders in the company? If not, take some steps to get connected to more people. Build a long-term strategy for each client. How will you go about developing more relationships within that firm?

Offer Existing Clients Additional Services

We often leave business on the table because we only meet one of our client's needs. I read an article years ago about McDonald's that got me thinking about how professional service providers can get more business from existing clients. McDonald's wanted to increase profits, but the company's employees were mostly students and part-timers who had no skin in the game for growing sales. So, McDonald's instructed every cashier to ask, "Do you want fries with that?" This method of asking for more business grew the bottom line by 20 percent globally.

Most of us aren't selling burgers and fries. But what would happen if we asked our clients, "What else can I do for you?" This simple question can be the difference between higher profitability and no opportunity at all.

I recommend doing more research about the organizations that you work with, perhaps even reading the company's annual report. The more you know about the challenges that company or client faces, including the client's long-term growth goals, the more you can find ways to help.

Likewise, many of us offer services that our clients don't know about. They don't know because we don't share enough about what we do! So, as you gain a better understanding of your clients' needs, ask them: "Do you want fries with that?" By doing your homework and understanding your clients' current and future needs, you can find ways to help them—authentically. That will increase your own bottom line.

The best part about working with an existing client is that new opportunities typically close 33 percent sooner than traditional prospecting. Because of your strong relational connections, you'll face less competition. Your profitability will skyrocket, as will the value that you bring to your client.

Epilogue

Business development, marketing, networking, sales, and relationship building are the most effective ways to grow your business. Unfortunately (I know from experience), most people dread that part of the job because they think they have to sell themselves in salesy, pushy ways.

Maybe you have been paralyzed by that view. Pitching your services is not what you signed up for. You worked hard for your degree and to build your experience, but selling yourself was not part of your plan. I understand that.

It's difficult for me to hear my clients say they are not able to pay their bills, that they can never get ahead, that they can't bring in enough business. It's also difficult to hear my clients who work in large companies say they might lose their compensation packages if they don't bring in enough new business. Some risk losing their jobs.

These are frightening scenarios. So, my mission is to provide tools that help professionals achieve their goals without being forced into impersonal, inauthentic molds. That's why I believe that focusing on people is more important than anything else.

Building relationships, being curious, and (of course) doing a great job will always lead to more.

If you don't make relational business development a priority, then your challenges will continue. You might be able to grow your business without investing in your network of relationships, but you will struggle to generate a consistent flow of referrals and new business—and to avoid the roller coaster ride we talked about earlier.

Think about how to build relationships wherever you go: at your HOA meetings, at your child's sports games, while serving on a board, at the gym, at networking events—it doesn't matter. Being mindful of the natural, authentic ways to connect with people and opportunities will ensure a prosperous and bountiful pipeline.

I invite you to start a relationship with me. Please visit my website and sign up for my monthly newsletter so we can stay in touch. You will also find resources to help you with your business development strategies.

By making small changes to the way you do business development, you will reap the benefits for the long-term. You'll have a profitable and stable business. You will not only support your career, but you'll increase your well-being and lower your stress.

What's stopping you from taking the first step?

Other books and resources by
Stephanie Wachman

Own Your Time: Professional Time-Management Strategies for a Profitable and Balanced Life
In this collection of succinct and practical chapters, Stephanie Wachman shares powerful and proven time-management strategies that restore balance and productivity to life. *Own Your Time* is a user-friendly reference that enables executives and professionals to reclaim control of their lives in a world full of distractions and stress.

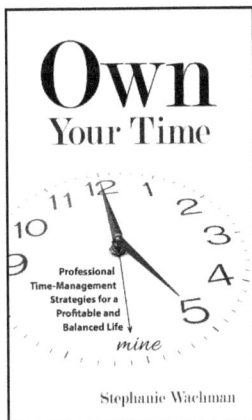

For further practical resources, bookmark Stephanie Wachman's website, *stephaniewachman.com*

www.ingramcontent.com/pod-product-compliance
Lightning Source LLC
Chambersburg PA
CBHW071434210326
41597CB00020B/3786